WHAT OF
DARDANELLES?

An Analysis

By
Granville Fortescue

Edited by John Wilson

Gosling Press

Foreward

Granville Fortescue had been an American soldier with the Rough Rider serving with his cousin Theodore Roosevelt. He was wounded at the San Juan Hill in Cuba in 1898 and served in the Philippines in the Spanish American war. He later served as a presidential aide in the first Roosevelt administration.

After this he was posted to Japan as a military attaché during the Russo Japanese war in 1904. Fortescue wrote for the Daily Telegraph during the first world war and latter during the Spanish Civil War.

As a neutral American he could travel in Turkey and was able to witness at first hand the situation from the Turkish perspective as well as knowing many of the journalists who were covering the campaign from the Allied side. His previous military experience and his time in Japan gave him a good insight to the issues of the campaign.

Published in 1915 before the end of the campaign this short publication lays bare many of the strategic issues of the campaign.

Map showing the minefields and main gun batteries in March 1915

WHAT OF THE DARDANELLES?

An Analysis

By
Granville Fortescue

INTRODUCTION

"You are the only man in England who knows the whole truth about the Dardanelles." When this remark was made to me by the chief of the greatest newspaper syndicate in England, it gave me pause and reflection. Was it true that the English public had but a faint conception of the obstacles the Dardanelles Army was endeavouring to surmount? Did the people of England ignore the difficulties of terrain, the lack of water, the enemy's scientific preparation for defence in their hope for rapid victory? Above all were they ignorant of the south-west gales, due in October, and their portent? Did they know that unless the enemy was decisively beaten before winter set in their wonderful army equal in soldierly qualities to the Spartans, would be marooned? With the coming of the gales, communication with the base of supplies would become precarious and fitful. Can men, even of heroic mould, fight without food and ammunition? What would be the fate of the Mediterranean Expeditionary Force if unsuccessful now? These and other thoughts kept fermenting in my mind.

When all measures taken in this war are weighed and analysed, it will be found that England's severest handicap has been undiscriminating censorship. Are the English averse from knowing the truth, be it bitter medicine? No people take "bad news" in a better spirt. It augers a total misunderstanding of the psychology of the British race to deem it necessary to deny them knowledge of the facts. And it is an insult to its intelligence to dose a full-grown, self-reliant nation on the pap accounts of spurious victories, "revolutions" in the enemy's domain and elaborations of false hopes, which is served out form Athens, Amsterdam and Rome. But the English people having been kept in darkness as to the actual conditions, and, at the same time fed on counterfeit news of the most hopeful nature, are suddenly called upon to make the most alarming sacrifices. Is it odd that they are bewildered? The censorship is responsible for the peculiar and wrong attitude of the people of England towards their army. The fighting force is regarded in the light of a championship football team. It sports the colours and carries the hopes of England, while the great mass of the nation acts the part of audience. The army is treated as a detached organisation in which the man in the street has only remote interest implied in paying taxes. In the present war this is woefully wrong. But people are not to blame for such a point of view. It is not their fault if they are not alive to their responsibilities. The pernicious result can be laid to the charge of censorship.

The menace of a graver peril lies in the use of this particular instrument. Cannot it be made the shield of inefficiency and incompetence? It were better not to dwell on this question.

It would be instructive to compare the originals of the despatches of my friend Mr. Ashmead Bartlett, with the text published in the press. This brilliant journalist and experienced military writer is not far wrong in his conclusions, even when he sees only one side of the Kriegspiel curtain. Having campaigned with Ashmead Bartlett at the siege of Port Arthur, and in Morocco, and being colleagues on the staff of the Daily Telegraph, I consider I can judge when his writings have been edited. In certain cases I believe this to have been the case in his Dardanelles dispatches. He does bring out the difficulties under which the English army is fighting, but he fails to open the eyes of his readers to the inordinate cost of overcoming those difficulties. His descriptive writing is at times entrancing, but his conclusions and comments on tactical operations are vague and sometimes wholly lacking. This is not in line with the character of this war correspondent. An uncensored critique on the Dardanelles campaign from Ashmead Bartlett would be very enlightening.

What did Mr Winston Churchill mean by his famous speech in which he declared the British Army at Gallipoli to be within a few miles of a most astounding victory? I forget the exact date of this statement, as I was in the Dardanelles at the time, but it must have been June, and here we are in October and the prophesy still remains to be fulfilled. The utterance under the circumstances was most perplexing. If it was put forth in an effort to bewilder the enemy, it certainly succeeded, for the Turkish commanders saw no weakness in their line. Someday the former First Lord will surely explain his words.

All this by way of preliminary. It is only introduced in this introduction to account for the befuddled conception of the real situation which exists in the mind of the average Englishman. This book is a modest effort to clear the atmosphere. My knowledge of the Dardanelles is derived from several sources. First I was thrown in with a certain military observer in Warsaw, for obvious reasons I cannot be more specific, who had passed through the Dardanelles several times in times of peace, and whose work was to make a special study of the defences so far as was feasible for a foreigner. Afterwards this gentleman acted as a military observer through the two Balkan wars. He prides himself upon being a professional soldier, and events have justified his judgements as outlined to me.

Next it was my fortune to find in Constantinople certain friends who have witnessed the first attempts to force the straits, and who have been on the ground during the actual bombardments. Two of these friends had special training in military matters. Lastly, I actually passed through the Dardanelles myself. I visited both the Gallipoli and the

Anatolian military zones. I saw the forts of Kilid Bahr and Chanak at close quarters. I rode down the coast to Kum Kale. I saw the British landing of May 25, the last of the Majestic, the River Clyde, the Turkish Howitzers in action, the battleship bombardments, and the lines of French, English and Turkish trenches at Seddul Bahr. I was an onlooker at the greatest military contest the world has witnessed. I tried to make a careful study of all I saw. Perhaps, as sometimes happens with an onlooker at a game of chess, I saw and observed fairly accurately the probable results of the moves of the antagonists. This analysis is an epitome of my observations.

Hythe, October, 1915

THE INITIAL BLUNDER.

ON the eighteenth of March, 1915, some British Marines bought fruit in the village of Krithea Then they left this collection of tumbledown Turkish houses, and made their way towards a towering hill that sloped up from the valley north and east of the town. It was hot. Somewhat out of condition because of several months of enforced inactivity, these "handy men" soon emptied their water bottles. Thirst quickly made the rough climbing an arduous adventure. A few of the sea soldiers sought water from the wells near the native houses. A glance into the turbid depths of liquid heavy with decaying animal matter discouraged the thought of replenishing water bottles here. With parched throats they went scrambling down a ravine, a fissure in the soil whose sides rose sharp above them, shutting out all the world save a patch of blue sky. They passed through this gully unconscious that the fates were preparing a dozen thrilling war dramas, each with its climax of heroism, staged within the narrow compass of the rock encrusted walls. Not the most imaginative amongst them in his wildest flights of fancy would have thought to call this gully the "string bean." Yet this band was peacefully passing through the "haricot."

A little beyond a trickling stream crossed the line of march. It was a tiny rill that would dry up rapidly under the coming suns of summer. As the marines thankfully filled their tins, some scooped the cool water up in their hands to assuage their thirst, they had no thought for the future destiny of that particular rivulet. Refreshed, these marines marched on out of the confining walls of the gully to a broad valley. It was like emerging from a tunnel. The sunlight streamed down upon them with the grateful warmth of spring. The valley led away to the north, rising and falling in gentle slopes like a heaving sea of green. Here and there the ground moulded

5

into regular hills, shapes that looked more like gigantic tumuli than the handiwork of Nature. Plane trees and Turkish oaks spotted the landscape, giving promise of welcome shade. New grass, thick with clover leaves, carpeted much of the soil. On the hillsides a heavy tangled brushwood grew. One of the marines said this brush-wood looked like gorse. But this Gallipoli gorse is thicker in branch, higher in growth, and more entangled than the English variety.

The marching was cooler now. The marines had the feeling of altitude; it was as if they trod a plateau. The sea, which seemed to drop off the edge of their world, shimmered beneath them in a plane two or three hundred feet lower. Suddenly the band found their path blocked by what one called "a crack in the face of the earth." It was a deep donga, that cut across the valley unsuspected and hidden. A detour took them round this, but farther marching showed these irregular fissures to be a feature of the terrain. A sub-lieutenant, in writing of this march later, described the land as "highly accidental." The towering hill that was the objective of the march dominated the landscape. It was a curious shape that arrested attention. From the highest central summit two minor hills shouldered out on either side, giving the formation a highly artificial appearance. And as is the case, whenever some special aspect of nature assumes an odd form, the beholders were unaccountably impressed. One travelled sea-soldier caught the whole impression in a happy comparison. "Looks like a Buddha I once see outside Yakahama, that blooming hill does. Wish we'd reach it."

In time they did, on the maps this queer hill is marked "Achi Baba".

It is with a twofold purpose that I have tried to reconstruct the march of this handful of marines sent ashore on the day the British and French battleships attempted their ill advised,

6

but heroic effort to force the Dardanelles. I wish to give my reader a first view of the physical difficulties of the country, difficulties that cannot be too highly emphasised, and I wish to bring out vividly the fact that a landing force, undertaken at the time indicated, would have changed the whole story of the Gallipoli campaign. A neutral officer who has been with the Turkish armies from the beginning of hostilities, assured me that three divisions disembarked on that fateful day in March might have marched triumphantly from the heel to the neck of the Gallipoli peninsula at Bulair. This statement was based upon a knowledge of the number of Turkish troops in the sector at that time, and their state of preparedness. A German officer confirmed this assertion. He argued that the loss of this opportunity stamped the British Staff. or those who planned the coup as men of mediocre military calibre.

It is not necessary to pay much heed to this bit of German bias, but an honest questioning on the plans of the High Command is imperative.

Why was no land attack planned in conjunction with the naval assault on the Dardanelles? Did the originator of the action believe that the fleet alone could force the passage and capture the land forts by the same manoeuvre? Anyone guilty of such miscalculation surely does need the curtain of the censorship behind which to hide. The whole question of the naval fight will be dealt with later. Here we are concerned only with the grave error of omitting land operations at a time when they would have, in all probability, brought partial if not complete success.

Were there no land forces available? The obvious retort to this is that under such conditions the naval assault should have been postponed. It is obvious to any student of this campaign that the British command started out with an imperfect knowledge of the conditions which confronted them. The few troops in the vicinity of Seddul Bahr and Kum Kale in mid-March would have been a mouthful for two resolute divisions. If any doubt at first that an army was essential to the success of the forcing of the Dardanelles, and the capture or destruction of the forts guarding the Narrows, later operations have thrown a clear light on this point. It is the lack of foresight shown by the mind that conceived the plan of smashing a channel through to the Black Sea which is appalling. This mind worked either in ignorance of the facts under serious misinformation, or in absolute contempt of all military and naval precedents. The latter is probably the fact.

What this folly baa cost England, aye, the whole British Empire, in blood has not yet been totalled. It would seem that the naval commanders, both English and French, were swept into the adventure by a masterful personality who held the lessons of all wars, naval and military, in contempt. If a force was not available on the 18th of March conditions absolutely dictated a delay. Little harm would result in a postponement. The element of surprise would still have been with the British if no bombardment had been inaugurated until all was in readiness for a joint comprehensive attack by sea and land. Three weeks would have been ample time in which to organise an expeditionary army of a size equal to the task at the time. It need not be argued that the Turks would have used those three weeks, as was later the case, in making the southern section of the Gallipoli almost impregnable. The Turk was not expecting a serious effort in this quarter at the time indicated. It was only after the fleet had failed that he quickly realised his vulnerability from the land side. Naturally he began with feverish energy to remedy the defect. How well he accomplished this I shall describe later.

There is one other explanation of this remarkable military mistake. It is contained in the remark made to me by an experienced English staff officer :

" We would have had the whole peninsula by this time" (the conversation took place in June) "if the Greeks had not let us down." I had heard much about that expected co-operation of the Greeks in the Dardanelles. I could see no reason for such co-operation, save a remote sentimental one. And the myths of Homer cannot be expected to urge the modern Greek to war. The amazing thing was that this officer saw nothing extraordinary in laying a British failure at the doors of Greece. How long will it be before England realises that her sons, not the French, the Russians, the Belgians, nor any other people problematically affected by the war, and her sons alone, carry the balance of victory on their shoulders? This shifting the blame to the Greeks is unworthy. Suppose twenty thousand troops were promised to assist the manoeuvres of the Allied fleets, this fact only emphasises the error in attempting the attack with battleships alone. It indicates that the High Command knew the value of a conjunctive plan of the land and sea forces, and disregarded it. When it was found that Greece was a broken reed, British transports should have received orders to carry their war freight to Gallipoli. Such a change of plan would involve no insuperable difficulty.

But this was not done. After a careful and serious study of the course of events in the Dardanelles, in my opinion the fact that the Allied fleets have not passed into the Sea of Marmora is primarily due to the initial blunder of challenging the passage of the Hellespont with ships alone,

The casualty lists that appear in the London papers from the Mediterranean Expeditionary Forces today are the result. It is the simple demonstration of the immutable Law of Cause and Effect. How this initial mistake will run through the whole of the English campaign in Turkey no one can as yet prophesy. Commanders are no longer free agents. A set of contingencies are staged that fetter the action of both antagonists. Instead of a short and glorious battle ending in triumph, we have a long-drawn-out trail of tragedy, glorious, indeed, in its proof of British heroism, but leading only to victory after taking a toll that spreads sorrow to the remotest confines of the Empire.

THE SECOND MISCALCULATION.

"Ships are unequally matched against forts in the particular sphere of fort ***. The quality of one is ponderousness, enabling great passive strength; that of the other is mobility."
ADMIRAL MAHN

THE forcing of the Dardanelles is a military problem of enthralling interest. It is an example, if I may coin the phrase, of intensive strategy. It combines almost all the elements upon which the whole theory of war rests. It promises political consequences that may run like a flood through the centuries. Whatever its results, the maps of Europe and Asia must be re-drawn when the struggle finishes. Here is the political nature of the war in this zone opening to our imagination a vision of consequences more stupendous than all the dreams of Alexander, Caesar, and Napoleon. Here is the last European citadel of the infidel attacked by the Christians. If the English and their Allies triumph, it will not be as conquerors seeking lands to hold in subjection, but rather as missionaries carrying the light of civilisation, the spark that was struck in France in 1702, into the gloom of Asia And there is always on the horizon of our imagination, as it plays about the future here, the misty outlines of occult Baghdad. State policy that has issued from the brains of Britain's greatest statesmen for nearly a hundred years bears relation, remote or intimate, upon the battling in progress along the Dardanelles today. It is essential that England win in this battling. How essential, the present generation cannot guess. In Turkey, in Egypt, in India, throughout the East, the sun of England will never shine so bright again if her soldiers fail in Gallipoli. The capture of the Narrows may hasten the climax of the war. Defeat will mean a dragging decade of tragedy.

The political side of the fighting in Gallipoli holds the mind of the politician. The military side absorbs the soldier. In a narrow circle he sees every element of modern military activity, by sea and by land, being tested. He sees the majestic super-Dreadnought pitted against the pestilent submarines. Battleships contending with forts. Shells of enormous size and force dropped on rabbit burrows. Aeroplanes circle like Sinbad's Roc overhead. Sausage-shaped balloons sway between sea and sky. Every weapon, from the mighty 15-in. gun that belches a ton of high explosive from its cavernous breach to the glittering hand bayonet is used. Every stratagem devised for fighting a civilised or uncivilised foe gets its trial. The battling on sea and land in the Dardanelles brings out every thrilling incident of combat between fort and ship, land force and land force, the whole set down in an environment pulsating with historic interest. The ruined walls of Troy look down on the rusty sides of the transport River Clyde. The hulk of the E 15 lies in the Hellespont. So does the fighting instinct bridge the cycles.

A certain strategist voiced the complete ignorance of all Britain on the subject of the Dardanelles in a number of his widely read periodicals. This paragraph appeared in February, I write in October. His views are thus expressed: - "The attack upon the Dardanelles is only indirectly a land operation. It is chiefly a naval operation with a naval object, and conducted in the main by naval forces."In the opinion of this strategist and war prophet, the line of the Gallipoli peninsula could be turned by anyone in command of the sea Once this was an accomplished fact, the reduction of the forts would be only a question of time, " with modern siege train and high explosives a question of what should be a short time."

I do not know if this gentleman is in the confidence of the Admiralty, or if he be the close friend of the former First Lord, but his complete misunderstanding of the Dardanelles problem is in line with what happened in the Narrows on the eighteenth of March, 1915. It would be interesting to know who is responsible for the premature and disastrous attempt to force the Dardanelles. Perhaps history will draw back the curtain which the censor has dropped before this personality. It would be instructive to learn on what grounds he hoped for success. How was he able to persuade highly trained and skilful technical naval officers to forget the lessons of the past, and all their own hardly acquired knowledge, in a hazard that was foredoomed to failure? Why did he brush aside the dictum of the most respected naval authority of modern days, whom I quote at the head of this chapter? Did he think that the inch added to the calibre of the guns in the Queen Elizabeth's batteries changed the status of a contest between ship and fort? Has that inch given the ship an advantage which permits it to attack the fort with impunity in the particular sphere of the latter? Results are far from confirming this hope.

Search as one may for sound reasons for the plan as executed, and you find none. I had an excellent opportunity to estimate the chances of success for a battleship running the gauntlet of the forts at the Narrows, and can state unequivocally that they are nil. What is more, I had been assured of this fact before I had ever seen the Dardanelles. Two neutral officers, whose business it had been to study conditions military and naval in Turkey, discussed the question, by and large, with me, and came to the identical conclusion. Thus it was to be inferred that the mind that planned the attack on the Dardanelles by sea alone must have acted upon information hidden from men who had made the problem a study. Unfortunately, if this was the case. that mind was misinformed.

What is more, the English people were sadly befooled. The question was put to me in London in March, "when I thought the Dardanelles would be forced ?" And my English friends laughed me to scorn when I answered; "Not within six months, and perhaps never." I gave this opinion under pressure. My military experience has taught me nothing is so uncertain as war. I am no war prophet.

One guess is as good as another, but a guess based upon even a limited knowledge of facts may sometimes come nearer the mark. But the prognostications of the Press at the time under discussion were simply beyond understanding. All England was told that the splendid Navy paused at the very door of victory. Panic sifted through Constantinople like the simoon, so said the papers. And the Press Bureau called no halt on these cruel deceptions.

England paid little heed to the ships lost in the preliminary reconnoitres. They were old and out of date. It was a little price to pay for the glorious victory that would follow from this sacrifice. The nation stood trembling in expectancy. I can give another picture. In Chanak, in one of the observation posts, two neutral correspondents with German leanings watched the sinking of the French ship Bouvet. The hill on which the control station stood overlooked the long funnel entrance to the Dardanelles. The war correspondents, with Zeiss binoculars glued to their eyes, watched in breathless suspense a succession of black dots that seemed propelled over the waters by volumes of black smoke.

Viewing the same alcove from a little better vantage point was a youngish good-looking man wearing a naval jacket, white slacks, and a fez. Before him on a table a map was spread. It was divided into rectangles like a draughts board, and spotted with odd hieroglyphics called by cartographers "conventional signs." On the plotted map in the section showing the narrowing outlines of the Straits appeared a number of tiny red ovals. The initiated know these red ovals as the conventional sign for mines. Where they fly-specked the map was a mine field. The correspondents and the German naval officer were waiting for the black dots with smoking funnels to enter that field.

They paid little attention to the shattering explosions that thundered up to their ears, so intense was their concentration. They noticed where the Turkish shells struck in the water about the approaching battleships, and kept sharp watch for a hit in a control top. This they did automatically while every perceptive faculty was focussed on the strip of blue water sown with the seed of destruction and death.

Nearer and nearer came the ships; greater and greater grew the noise of gun fire. Still the three men waited watching. The facial muscles of one of the correspondents began an anxious twitching under the strain. The officer ran his tongue over his dry lips and muttered in guttural. With glasses still fixed on the oncoming warships, one hand groped about on the map for a pair of compasses. Suddenly his hand stopped as if paralysed. His eyes saw a great jet of spray and smoke shoot up from the sea under the bow of a battleship. It listed immediately, keeping on the circle of its course.
"She's got hers!" shouted one of the correspondents.
A smile of relief crept into the eyes of the German officer.
" Those damned English ships are done. They cannot pass our mine fields."
Then the neutral correspondents with pro-German leanings showered their companion with congratulations. One ventured a cordial slap on the back. Although a minor royalty, the German officer did not resent this.

The mine fields make the Dardanelles Straits impregnable. In spite of the four knot current that flows steadily down these waters, the mines have been most scientifically placed and solidly anchored. They are expected to defy the grapplings of the most powerful mine sweepers. It takes twenty-six mines to close the channel completely. These mine lines are run in parallels, the mines of the second line being opposite the intervals of the first. The breadth of the field varies. The only successful method of attacking a mine field is with what are called "mine sweepers," powerful steam tugs fitted with cranes and grappling irons used in removing the floating explosive buoys.

In the Dardanelles the mine fields are protected against the operations of the mine sweepers, not only by the guns of the various batteries and forts that line the hills on either side of the channel, but by carefully hidden redoubts and gun emplacements along the shore. These positions command the waters above the mine fields at point blank range. Thus in the Narrows, where the main mine fields are situated, it is impossible for the "sweepers" to work.

Considering this one feature alone of the Dardanelles defences, why should the ships of the Allied fleets attempt, an adventure certain to end in disaster? I have seen it stated that the attack on the Dardanelles was simply a naval demonstration; that no serious effort was made to force the Straits, and as an exposition of English and French sea power the sacrifice of the Ocean, Irresistible, and Bouvet was justifiable. This "saving one's face" is nonsense. The one thing demonstrated by the naval action was the strength of the Turkish defences.

The result filled the German commanders and the subordinate Turkish officers manning these defences with a confidence no development has since been able to disturb.

The whole operation was as unfortunate as it was unnecessary.

What induced the High Command to send their vessels into jeopardy? After sifting the probabilities, the only reasonable answer to this question is found in the success of the Fleet operations on February 19. With guns that far outranged the batteries of Seddul Bahr Fort and Kum Kale, the ships fired salvo after salvo with the precision and safety of target practice. The concrete of the forts was pulverised. Shells dropped on Seddul Bahr from every point of a semi-circle of which it was the centre. Meanwhile the shells of the Turkish guns fell a thousand yards short of the ships. Naturally, the Turks abandoned their positions in the face of such an unequal contest and under such an unprecedented bombardment.

Yet when the landing parties sent ashore from the ships examined the silenced forts, they were surprised at the character of the damage sustained. The concrete and stone construction of the forts alone suffered. Earthworks showed trifling scars. Even the great shells of the Queen Elizabeth burst off the thick clay banks ineffectively. The landing parties found it difficult to destroy completely these unconsidered defences.

No doubt the moral of the Turkish garrisons touched the bottom of the glass barometer under these bombardments. The situation was hopeless. What was the use of trying to fight an enemy whom your shells could never touch? So the defenders abandoned the forts and sought refuge beyond the range of the searching shells.

This easy victory warped the judgment of the naval Commanders. The fact that the Turks practically ran away under the rain of iron fragments misled the Allied Admirals.

It must have made them hope for the same result in an attack on the forts within the entrance. If they reasoned thus, they reckoned without their host.

Having passed through the Dardanelles and spent some time on both the Gallipoli and Asiatic sides of the Straits, I venture a description of the defences. I have traversed the coast from Fort Nagara to within a short distance of the Kum Kale. I have examined the forts and batteries at Kilid Bahr. I have studied the positions commanded by Fort Dardanos. With my own eyes I have seen the mine sweepers working while Turkish howitzers launched shells at their decks. The German-Turkish plan to foil the fleets was unfolded before me. Here it is.

Since the attacks in February, the European and Asiatic shores of the Dardanelles have been turned into two great fortresses. Instead of dividing these shores into named defences as Medejieh, Chimilik, Kilid Bahr, Dardanos, Kum Kale, and so forth, or giving them designating letters, as do the Admiralty communiques, consider them as two linked-up lines of defences, paralleling the narrow passage through which the ships must venture. All points offering suitable fields of fire have been crowned with batteries. The banks of the Straits fairly bristle with guns. Not that you see them sticking out from the hillsides like cannon from a warship turret. Redoubts, emplacements, and gun pits are most carefully concealed. Experienced spotters at any distance save the shortest ranges can only locate the hidden guns by their flash. Aviators are completely baffled. If we except the movable howitzer batteries, artillery of large calibre is not found in these minor defences. They are supplied with an uncounted number of field and machine-guns. These latter play an important role in the defences, as I shall explain.

What I am trying to unfold is the thoroughness of the German-Turkish preparations. Every contingency is foreseen and provided for. Every span of the surface of the waters of the Straits is covered by a dozen guns.

Not only have the gun positions been enlarged and improved, but supplementary military works have been elaborated. New roads have been built. Better observation stations established. The whole transport system reorganised. In fact, the German touch shows everywhere. Much of this preparation strikes even the casual observer. But even more than one can guess goes on behind the fortress walls. Naturally this is a preparation not open to inspection. How the individual forts along the Narrows daily become a great menace to the ships that might attempt the passage of the Narrows did show on the face of things. New faces appeared among the garrisons - faces which neither fez nor turban could disguise their Teuton origin. The transports carrying these German artillerymen came with holds filled with ammunition. Great heavy boxes were lightered ashore and trundled through the gates of the forts. If you were familiar with ammunition cases, you guessed the contents of these boxes.

This factory of preparation seems to have escaped the observation of the High Command or else they ignored it. They had undoubtedly accurate information as to the position and armament of the Dardanelles defences. But did they take thought of the German touch when they sent their old ships, manned by plenty of young men, through the gamut of those guns?

The forts that guard the Narrows from Nagara and Kilia to Kilid Bahr and Chanak are not in a strict sense modern. This fact in a measure contributes to their strength. Earth and not concrete is the basis of construction. It has been demonstrated that against properly constructed earthworks the effect of the highest power shell is slight. In the bombardments directed against the forts of the Narrows by the Queen Elizabeth, the Agamemnon, Lord Nelson, and others, 15 and 8-in. shells burst harmlessly on the glacis of the different defences. The forts are all built along the same lines. The walls of riveted earth are raised about 30 ft. above the foundation, and are about twice as deep as they are high. All forts are scientifically faced. Usually there are eight embrasures in each face with a 6-in. gun in each. These guns are not modern. They cannot be fired with the rapidity of the latest design fortress artillery, but against vessels cruising in the narrow passage they command, a round in two minutes, which they are capable of developing with German taught gunners, is amply sufficient.

Of course, these guns have not the range of the ordnance mounted in the battleships. What advantage is gained from this is nullified because the ships must engage in the narrow walled-in channel of the Dardanelles. It is not more than three-quarters of a mile from shore to shore at the narrowest point of the Strait. This is roughly the distance that separates Chanak from Kilid Bahr. From Fort Kephes to Baikrah battery, where the mine fields are laid, there is two and a half miles of water. Connect these four points in a quadrilateral, and you have a veritable canon of death.

A ship entering this zone is in danger from three sides. Below her keel are the treacherous mines, while her broadsides are the targets for the innumerable guns that line both banks of the channel. She is exposed to attacks from above, for not infrequently Turkish aeroplanes attempt to drop bombs on the decks of the vessels. How could it be expected that any hostile craft would live through such a fire as could be developed here?

Much was expected from the indirect fire poured into this zone by the Queen Elizabeth. Her giant batteries were directed against the forts at Kilid Bahr and Chanak. Aeroplanes "spotted" for the ships' gunners. Yet with this assistance the results were insignificant. In the first place, the forts and batteries on the European side of the Straits lie under the lee of the Gallipoli cliffs, in a dead angle, and of the thousands of projectiles expended only two landed directly in gun embrasures.

There is one more point I wish to bring out in dwelling on the handicaps under which ships attack forts in the Dardanelles Straits. The fire control station is the eye of a battleship. It is usually located on the foretop, from which point the optic nerves, navy-phones and speaking tubes, lead to the brain of the battleship in the conning tower. The registering faculties are some under-officers and sailors perched in this cage a hundred foot above the waves. It follows that if you destroy the eye of a ship you render it useless. It is just this that the minor fortifications lining the shore of the Strait have for their object. The sailorman may laugh at the field batteries and the one-pounders hidden in the brush, and look on their shells as simple flea-bites on his armoured sides, yet these small shells, if they hit their mark, will destroy a control station. The " eye " of the ship is the target of the Turkish gunners.

I will not go further into the preparations made for strengthening the Dardanelles defences after the destruction of the forts at Cape Helles and Seddul Bahr. I cannot state with certainty if there are stations for launching land torpedoes. The officer supposed to have the establishment of such stations as his work assured me that they did not exist. He would give me no information about floating mines either. However, it can be taken for granted that if such expedients are practical, the German-instructed Turks are using them.

When we know that under ordinary circumstances a ship is no match for a fort in the sphere of the fort, how could the ships of Britain be poured into this funnel of fortifications? Was there not some radical miscalculation chargeable against someone? British sailors will sail their ships down the Styx to the gates of Hell if they are so ordered, but would the probable results justify any First Lord in ordering such a manoeuvre?

THE LAND DEFENCES.

British history has no more brilliant page than the story of the fighting in the Dardanelles. Thousands of men have touched the highest level of heroism in the battles that raged back and forth across the cliffs and gorges of Gallipoli. Bravery is a byword. Self sacrifice has become an eagerly sought privilege. No one can write of the unflinching courage, the unwavering devotion to duty, the uncomplaining suffering of the Allied troops in the Dardanelles without being fulsome.

Overcoming the friction, as Clausewitz calla it, of the expedition was a marvellous achievement. Here the British Navy showed its worth. The magnitude of the task would have appalled less resolute minds. But the Navy, long accustomed to doing Britannia's work in any corner of the seven seas, tackled the unheard of proposition as if it were all in the day's work. Troopships came from the fringes of the Empire. Leviathan liners from England, commandeered cattle ships from the Antipodes, ancient transports from India, all filled with precious human freight that had to be protected from the lurking submarines.

The monster fleet that crowded Mudros Bay was an object lesson of England's might. The heterogeneous collection of humanity that was carried by this fleet was a proof of Imperial solidity. Yet the fact of that fleet is the very weakness of the whole expedition. It indicates the longest and most insecure line of communications over which any army was ever supplied. Of course there are advanced operation bases at Malta, Alexandria, Lemnos; but every man, every shell, every cartridge expended in the operations against the Gallipoli fortifications comes from England or some of her outlying possessions. From the military point of view, history can show no parallel for this undertaking.

While filled with admiration for the splendid daring of the idea of forcing the Dardanelles by a land attack, yet we must pause to inquire if it offered any reasonable chance of success. The promoters of the plan hoped for the speedy and spectacular surrender of Stamboul. The attacks of the Allied ships were now a recognised failure. The capture of the forts from the land side was the only chance of clearing the passage of the Dardanelles. Obviously a land attack must be tried, or the expedition abandoned.

Surprise, one of the greatest elements of success in military operations, was lost. It would seem that the lesson of the German touch, as exemplified by the improvement of the defences of the Straits, was forgotten when the English commander proposed to get astride of the peninsula Certainly he did not expect the systematic organisation of defence that has met all his attacks. Obviously he did not know, or he underrated, the difficulties that beset the most insignificant movement of troops in this sector. Turkish battalions camped on lateral and longitudinal communications waiting for the English. They had prepared the ground.

The greatest objection to the Gallipoli plan of campaign as developed was that it gave the Turks all defensive advantages. They were fighting over country where they knew every contour of the ground. Their lines of communication were safe. If they were driven in, every attack would result in consolidating the positions they already held. Above all, the peninsula was itself a natural citadel.

It is most difficult to convey a correct impression of the terrain here in words. In order to comprehend intelligently the advantage of position and the tremendous superiority it gave the Turks, it is necessary to describe the peculiarities of the peninsula, bit by bit. Viewed from the sea, the salient feature of the landscape are the cliffs. These rise sheer from the water to two or three hundred feet. They have some reminiscent aspect of the coast about Dover. The face of these cliffs is a mixture of sandstone and clay. They are extremely irregular and, for the most part, difficult of ascent. The cliff sides are dotted irregularly with heavy brushwood and sometimes crowned with the same growth. This brushwood affords the defenders admirable cover. It is also a formidable natural obstacle.

Throughout the greater length of the coast line the configuration of the cliffs is such as to forbid any attempt at landing. Here and there a flat circle of land juts out from the base of the cliffs. On these beaches, as they are called, the different units of the attacking force were disembarked. In a flash they were swept by a hurricane of shell and shot. Picture, if you can, these men, loaded with kit, scaling the cliffs.

Beyond the shore line the land was a jumble of hill, ravine, gully, cleft, tableland, valley, and mountain. It was as if Nature had stored here all the odds and ends of contours not used in other parts of the earth. The hills have no system, and the nullahs wander in and out crossing and turning aimlessly. Yet the slopes of the hills provide exceptional fields of fire. It would seem as if the whole peninsula had been hastily built as an improvised fortress. Every summit, every chasm makes for impregnability. Nature is Turkey's first ally.

Strong as is this bulwark of Nature, no day passes but it is made artificially stronger. With the devilish ingenuity of long practice, the German military engineers have turned every ridge into a fort, every valley into a field of obstacles. Remember that this work commenced immediately after the attempt of the Allied ships to force the Straits. Day and night it has been carried on under the best instruction, from March until to-day. And it still proceeds. Even during the weeks of early reconnaissance, when Sir Ian Hamilton was working out the details of his plan, time and again he found it necessary to alter decisions already taken, because the outline of Gallipoli changed over night. Under the cover of darkness, the crest of a hill that offered protection to the attackers would disappear. In a week a gorge by which invaders might approach would be filled in. Marvellous is the only adjective that can describe the transformation.

But the Turks did not stop at altering contours. While trench building went on in feverish haste and the field of fire was everywhere improved, other detachments of sappers devoted their energies to erecting obstacles. In this work they put their main trust in wire. The transport that carried me from Stamboul to Chanak was holdful of bread and barb-·wire. Such are the staples of war. The Turks began weaving a network of wire entanglements completely around Gallipoli in March, and the work was practically completed before the first British soldier set foot on shore.

The barb-wire is a particularly tough and vicious manufacture. It is specially designed to resist the sharpest cutters. The peculiar nature of the country makes it possible to erect extensive fields of wire entanglements where they are not only safe from shell fire, but also hidden from the view of the attacking troop. This factor accounts for the very large percentage of casualties in all the Dardanelles operations. It is a military axiom that unprotected troops should never be thrown against intact wire entanglements. One has only to read carefully the graphic reports of Sir Ian

Hamilton to get a vivid picture of the havoc wrought in the British ranks because of the necessity of charging over country thick with this kind of obstacle.

It is not necessary to enumerate all the other barriers erected against any possible attack. Every device known to the military field engineer has been made. What I wish to emphasise particularly is the fact that this elaborate preparation took place after the naval attack of March 18. Not only did the High Command ignore the tremendous difficulties of land operations in this sector, but they greatly underrated the character of the troops defending it. Because the Turks were roughly handled in the Balkan Wars, certain military critics believed them to be inferior soldiers. This, since the Germans have taken charge of their instruction, is not the fact. I have seen the results of the German training of the Turkish Army from the instruction of infantry recruits to the making of trained artillerists, and nothing could be more thorough. There has never been any question of Turkish bravery. What has roused this bravery to its highest pitch is the fact that Turkey is invaded. The turbanned thousands that fill the trench lines in Gallipoli feel they are fighting for their homes and their religion. With this incentive, they do not have to be driven to the encounter by German officers as is currently reported. There may have been occasions when the lines have broken under impetuous British onslaughts, when it became necessary to resort to extreme measures in order to prevent panic; but any officer or soldier who has been in action in the Dardanelles will testify to the courage of the Turk.

At the time of the first landing, the Turkish forces outnumbered the British two to one. The result of the fighting that took place during the last week in April showed that the Allied forces could make no progress on the peninsula, unless heavily reinforced. This meant another long delay. In the month that followed, before these reinforcements were available, the Turk further improved and strengthened his line of fortifications. Here was another miscalculation, and one which affected the operations of the Allied forces in France and Flanders.

Another great disadvantage under which the Allied staff worked was the inferiority of their maps. Until the time they were fortunate enough to capture a, large-scale Turkish staff map of the Gallipoli peninsula, they were working in the dark. Anyone having the slightest military training knows what a fatal handicap this is.

I must mention another most serious drawback to prolonged operations in Gallipoli, especially during the summer months. Water is scarce. This elemental necessity has, in many instances, to be supplied from the transports. It needs no elaboration to indicate how this affected the already over-burdened supply system. I shall have occasion to refer again to the enormous difficulties of transports and its bearing upon possible final results.

In spite of the many difficulties under which Sir Ian Hamilton's army operated early in June, I consider that he had a gambler's chance of success. This chance was based upon possible exhaustion of the Turkish ammunition. At that time the Turkish Landsturm forces were armed with old-fashioned Remington rifles. What was the actual number of rounds per man available at the time I do not pretend to state; but from certain reliable sources I know that it was limited. Here, again, however, we overlooked the German touch. The train that carried me to Constantinople had all the second-class compartments filled with Germans. A glance told me they were not soldiers; a little observation indicated that they belonged to the mechanic class. It was not long before I discovered that these men were trained munition workers on their way to take over the ammunition factories of Turkey. As soon as the German system was inaugurated the three principal Turkish factories were turning out small arms ammunition in sufficient quantities to supply all the needs of the troops in Gallipoli. For the use of the Turkish Army it is not necessary to make the enormous high explosive shells which are absolutely necessary in the other theatres of war. On the Turkish side the principal weapons are the rifle, the machine-gun, and the hand-grenade. The native ammunition factories, under German supervision, have no great difficulty in supplying these weapons. They can also provide the small shells used by the field artillery. I believe that the large howitzer shells could not be made in Turkey in the early stage of hostilities. It is possible, however, that by this time the Germans have remedied this.

Appalling as the list of Turkish advantages which I have set down appears, yet in a way they are only secondary. In Gallipoli the greatest elemental factor of defence is the same as possessed by England. The peninsula is almost surrounded by water. Fortunately, the Allies have the naval strength that easily gives them the superiority in these waters. But in spite of this superiority the very fact that Gallipoli is almost an island makes the task of any invasion extremely hazardous. It is physically impossible to establish an absolutely safe line of communications. Reinforcements, ammunition, food, in fact all the sustenance of the army must be first collected and embarked in England, then transported to the base of operations, here it is either landed and stored as a reserve supply or sent directly to the zone of activities. Under protection of the battleships the transports approach the coasts. Soon they are under shell fire. At the same time a submarine may be lurking in the depths below them. Submitting to these risks, they must unload into lighters and small boats. There is not a practical landing-place at any point along the coast line. Morto Bay has been improved somewhat by the sinking of piers but conditions are far from being satisfactory. The lighters and small boats filled with troops or supplies, as the case may be, are now rowed ashore. If the operation takes place in day-light the tows are subjected to a gruelling shell and machine-gun fire. I have actually seen tows coming ashore with salvos of shrapnel bursting above them, and the water spotted all about with a hail of lead. In rough weather the difficulties are increased ten-fold. If the operation is attempted at night there is always the chance of the pinnace commander losing their bearings.

Bear in mind that the fighting force is dependent upon this precarious line of supply or its existence. If it is interrupted the troops perish. When its source of supplies are cut off an army has three alternatives: It may retire, surrender or fight until the last man is killed. There is no need to emphasise further the importance of communication. British naval supremacy guaranteed this line.

The Fleet was to perform another important military function. The battleship guns were to be the artillery of the expedition. They were to clear the way for the landing of the infantry. It was expected that the great naval shells would actually pound down the cliff-sides.

Actually the effect of these projectiles was small. Unless a fortunate shot landed within the narrow confines of a two feet wide trench, the shell burst harmlessly against the unyielding earth, or went whizzing over into Asia. And it was almost impossible for the naval aviators to locate the Turkish batteries. Unless the flyers could actually spot an enemy position a bombardment took on that character of gun fire called "shelling the woods."

One of the extraordinary phenomena of this war is the practical immunity of troops in trenches from the effects of shell fire. I have seen the hillsides covered with a haze of smoke from exploding projectiles, the earth reeking with lyddite gases. Deafening explosions follow one upon the other in one steady roll of thunder. Such a bombardment seems to promise certain annihilation to all caught within the shell-swept zone. Yet let the shelling cease, and send in the infantry against the position that one thinks must have disintegrated under the hail of iron, and whole battalions come to life from the section where the shells fell thickest. These resurrected soldiers meet the advance with a murderous fire. How they lived through the bombardment is one of the mysteries of modern warfare.

The ineffectiveness of the naval demonstrations was due in measure to the character of the shell used. These were of peculiar construction, specially adapted for armour piercing. Near Kilid Bahr a German marine with the characteristically interrogative bent of his race gathered a pile of fragments of a large shell. From these he had endeavoured to reconstruct a 15 in. projectile fired from the main batteries of the Queen Elizabeth. By actual count the case had smashed into eight fragments, varying in size from a bit as large as your hand to a sliver as long as a leg-bone. Besides these eight pieces the solid nose and base made up the complete shell. For the work in hand this type of ammunition has but limited value.

When an enemy battery or gun was definitely located, however, the battleship batteries made short work of silencing it. In this way the position of the troops on shore was made tenable. Unfortunately, the range of the naval guns was circumscribed. The configuration of the ground makes it a simple matter to hide batteries on the hillsides where the battleships' guns cannot reach them.

Also when an enemy battery is spotted, and things become too uncomfortable it is moved to a new position. This gave the Turkish artillery a special advantage in meeting all attacks.

Again it was difficult to keep up uninterrupted communication between ship and shore. This hampered fire control.

The howitzer batteries concealed on the Asiatic side of the Straits are another factor of defence. Their situation and mobility make them almost immune from the ships' fire, and if discovered by some sharp-eyed aviator in his hydroplane, their position is changed over night. They serve a double purpose. First, they protect the channel of the Dardanelles, and second, they can drop shot into the camps of the British and French. This is most demoralising. When troops are brought back for a, respite from the strain of battle, it is highly enervating to find the resting place under bombardment. The irritation of the men is increased when it is impossible to discover the enemy and give him a bit of his own medicine.

This sort of fire is especially disturbing to the wounded. As a rule, a man's nervous system fails him after he has been hit. Being carried back from the trenches, especially through the ravines in Gallipoli, is agony for the wounded. Picture a man who has been hit by a shell or peppered by a machine gun lying on the operation table of a field hospital after such a trip, and as the surgeon bends over him to have a howitzer shell explode before the door of the tent. Try and imagine the mental anguish of that man.

A question I asked myself time and again as I rode down to Kum Kale was, Why were the operations against the Asiatic coast of the Strait abandoned? Granting there was any hope for a land attack on the Gallipoli peninsula, it was imperative to protect the flanks. Leaving the Turks in undisputed control of the Anatolian shore gave them a base from which it was a simple matter to operate against the forces attacking across the Straits.

I saw a number of encampments along the valley of the Simois river from which it would be possible to bring troops into action in a flank attack. But the main reason for taking this section of the battle line was the destruction of the shore batteries.

I shall conclude this description of the Turkish preparations for defence by mentioning the most important factor in the plan. This is the machine gun. The conditions were ideal for the use of this weapon. Guns lined the trenches. They were sunk in the dongas. They were hidden in caves in the cliffs. This single type of arm has done more to hold back the British than any other weapon. Whole battalions have melted under its fire. Besides being wonderfully effective, it used the simplest kind of ammunition to manufacture. Here was an added advantage. No matter how many thousands of belts of cartridges were expended, others were quickly supplied to make good the waste. All the circumstances I have enumerated contributed in some degree to the checking of the attackers, but in my opinion the final balance in the scale of success was due to the machine guns. If it were possible to count and classify all the hits made by the defenders in the Gallipoli fighting, I feel sure that by far the larger percentage would be found to be casualties from machine-gun bullets.
I have here set down the conditions of war in Gallipoli in their naked simplicity. My reader can draw his own conclusions.

CONSEQUENCES.

In this analysis it is not necessary to go into the tactical details of the landings. The plan of invasion was such an elaborate one that it could not have been carried through without friction. The expedient of the River Clyde was a brilliant idea. Unfortunately, the idea was not well executed. There were minor miscalculations that interfered with the landings on other beaches. But incidents of this nature are to be expected in the execution of any complicated plan. All the checks suffered by the landing forces only served to bring into higher relief the courage and resourcefulness of the personnel. The bravery of British soldier and sailor has won the admiration of the world.

But success is not grounded alone in ability to fight. The Science of War implies a higher quality. It is a well recognised principle of all fighting that the simpler the plan, the more chance it has of insuring victory. Yet the conditions of the Dardanelles precluded a simple plan. I have already said that Nature is the Turk's first ally.

In the opinion of some military critics, the plan of attack as executed in the Dardanelles, weighing all the factors present, never offered more than a remote chance of success. It seemed to be directed against the very points where the Turks were strongest. The Germans considered the attempt to take Achi Baba as suicidal. As one officer expressed it, points of attack could not have better suited General Lyman Von Sanders, if he had chosen them himself. This must, have resulted from ignorance of the true nature of conditions.

Were there any alternative plans that offered more chance of success for this long-delayed attack?

There were two: First, the inauguration of operations north of Bulair with the cutting of the Gallipoli line of communications as its decisive point. Considering the enormous number of troops finally sent to the Dardanelles zone, operations on a large scale would have offered a reasonable hope of victory. Certainly the nature of the country north of Bulair is much more favourable for military operations than the bottle-like extremity of the peninsula

There was yet another plan. An invasion of the Anatolian coast offered certain advantages. Here also the country is less accidental than it is on the peninsula From Chanak south to Kum Kale, the ground is rolling, open, and partly wooded. The marshes of Schamander might have been a serious obstacle during the rainy season, but this difficulty being overcome, an invading force would have considerable freedom of movement. A few miles in from the coast a ridge parallels the line of the Straits. This ridge commands nearly all the coast line defences which are open to the rear. The forts at Chanak would be the objective of these operations.

Against this plan it has been urged that the forts on the Gallipoli side of the Narrows command those on the Asiatic side. This is true, yet were the Chanak forts taken, the troops holding them would be in position to destroy the mine fields. With the mines out of the way, the Allied fleets could pass into the Marmora.

There is little to be gained from reviewing the might-have-beens. The question of the moment is, what shall be the next course of action.

There is a rumour current that the Suvla Bay assault was within an ace of succeeding. It is asserted that if certain divisions had been reinforced at a critical moment they might have maintained themselves in a commanding position. This position has been indicated to me. If it is any consolation, I can assure those who think that the capture of the ridge in question would have ended the fighting, that such is not the case. But this is past history. We must concern ourselves energetically with the present.

Is there any chance of maintaining the troops in their present position until a new offensive can be inaugurated? What would be gained by such a course? These and other questions come at once to mind.

Seddul Bahr must be held at all costs. How this is going to be done is a problem that should hold the combined mental energies of all concerned.

Seddul Bahr is a key position in the Dardanelles. Some day it may be more important than Gibraltar. Holding this point, England commands the entrance to the Black Sea

For political reasons the few miles that have been so dearly won across the toe of the peninsula must be held. This will be no easy task. Seddul Bahr must be supplied against a siege. The defences will have to be consolidated and made impregnable. Winter quarters will have to be erected. Hospitals must be built and furnished. An enormous amount of reserve supplies and ammunition must be stored.

Landing stages can be built at Morto Bay. Ships unloading here will be under shell fire, but unless another point offers better protection against the storms, this risk must be run.

To complete the enterprise everything necessary will have to be brought from England. Every article carried on the Quarter-master and Commissary requisitions, from pins to portable houses, must be supplied. It will be a huge enterprise, but it is the only method of saving something from this historic blunder.

There is a hopeful feature in the problem, the Turkish soldier is not strongly effective in attack. Unless their ammunition were exhausted, he would never be able to drive the English out of the trenches they now hold. The defenders of Seddul Bahr could beat off all assaults as long as their cartridges held out. And these assaults could only be delivered along a narrow front.

I think the British can meet all trials. I base this belief on the wonderful endurance and dogged determination displayed by the Anzac divisions.

Holding Seddul Bahr will have a wide influence on the future of the British Empire. No man alive today can visualise what the command of the entrance to the Black Sea will mean in the coming decades. Seddul Bahr is a geographical point around which the future history of the world may revolve. It is a sacred duty to the dead whose bones lie bleaching in the brush of Gallipoli to hold this point for England.

THE SITUATION IN TURKEY.

The rumours of a revolution in Turkey have been so many and frequent that I must state they have not the least foundation in fact. Why should the British public be fed on those silly canards? Time and again I have read long despatches from Athens and Mytilene which purport to describe the troubled conditions in Turkey. I remember one item that told of a riot in Constantinople. Reference was made to the looting of the Pera Palace Hotel by a "stop-the-war" mob. On the date mentioned in the despatch I was stopping in this hotel. The whole story was pure invention. Personal observation convinced me that Constantinople was the most normal of all the capitals of the nations at war.

The routine of existence is but slightly affected by the tremendous efforts put forth in the military sphere. It were idle to imply that the arrival of thousands of wounded in the Turkish capital produced no reaction upon the populace. The Turks understand the symbolism of the wounded soldier. But they are no cravens. And they are confident that they are holding their own. It has been the pleasant task of the German officers present to explain with much detail the colossal error of the operations in the Dardanelles. When day after day the German equations are proved on the field of battle, it is small wonder that the banner of the Star and Crescent floats above a people serene in confidence of ultimate success.

The Ottoman Turks are not a people to be despised. They have not advanced along the paths of civilisation as have many other nations, but they have their ideals and standards. Travel has developed in me the habit of trying to estimate the moral worth of the countries I have seen. The moral worth of the great mass of Turks is not below that of many peoples considered far more civilised.

If any proof of the status of the Turks were needed, we have it in the mutual respect developed by the men of the opposing forces fighting in Gallipoli. It is war without enmity. No soldier worthy of the name can meet an honourable foe without admitting his fair qualities. This is what has happened in the Dardanelles. Even here in England I have failed to notice any active animosity towards the Turks.

It is interesting to trace the process which has led from the assassination of an Austrian prince to the war between England and Turkey. What brought Turkey into the war? This is a question I have been asked frequently. One answer is, the ambition of the Young Turkish party. The clever German played upon this ambition, at the same time fanning the flame of the fear of Russia which has existed in every Moslem heart for centuries. The clique headed by that extraordinary character, Enver Pasha, in forwarding their own ambition, have been the willing tools of German diplomatists. Though it may have failed in other capitals, German diplomacy was a complete success in Constantinople.

What has been promised the Turk for his aid in helping the schemes of the Teuton Emperor we can only guess at. Possibly Egypt.

As events are proceeding, there is now no chance of a revolution in Turkey. Yet should things go badly with the Army, the Enver Pasha Government would fall in a night.
The mental condition of the Turk who has studied in Europe and who does not belong to the political world is complete bewilderment. He had strong friendly feelings towards England. He was in sympathy with the French. No quarrel or

basis of disagreement existed with either country. Yet he finds his land invaded by the soldiers of both these nations. Here is the incentive for the present Turkish resistance. Patriotism in the Sultan's realm is not alone rooted in a love of country, but also springs from the strong religious faith that tinges national existence.

One particular theory that appeared constantly in the English papers dealt with the supposed friction that existed between the Turkish and the German officers. This was pure invention. I had the chance of seeing the relations between the officers, and they were working harmoniously for one end, the defeat of the British. The characteristic attitude of the German officer was offensive to the well-bred Turk, but this gentleman was intelligent enough to realize this must be overlooked. Turkey needed the brains of these arrogant aliens. On occasion natural jealousy showed in the accounts of victories. I remember that the Turkish communique recording the sinking of the Triumph and the Majestic implied that the Turkish Navy had a part in the accomplishment. Also the social relations existing between the officers of the two nationalities were non-existent. But to exaggerate these minor differences into serious friction was absurd. What is more, it deluded the English public.

I have said that during the period of my stay in Turkey, in May and June, conditions were almost normal. At one time this calm was disturbed. When the English submarines became so active in the Marmora, Constantinople made various anxious speculations as to the results that might ensue from the raids. But the slight excitement died quickly. It was shown that the lines of communication could not be permanently affected by the sinking of a few transports. Besides, a new road down the peninsula was opened immediately.

At one time there was momentary uneasiness about manufacturing the supply of ammunition for the troops in the Dardanelles. With the arrival of specially imported munition mechanics from the Essen factory all worry on this score passed.

At no time has there been any indication of a shortage of food. All private accumulations of coal have been reserved for the use of the Government, but this does not mean that the entire supply is depleted. I was informed that a Decauville railroad line had been run to the coal fields since the sea route had been blocked.

I have tried to set down a true epitome of the situation in Turkey, without flower of speech. Such were the conditions as I saw them. A normal people living as normal a life as a state of war allowed. All were confident. If they were certain of ultimate victory then, what must be their feelings now at the dramatic turn affairs have taken in the Balkans? What supreme effort can destroy this confidence?

THE BALKAN INFLUENCE.

The Balkan crisis comes at an opportune time. The evacuation of the Dardanelles zone can now be excused as a military necessity. He who pushed the plan can escape the indictment of his folly. In the East what would have been a blow to British prestige can be explained away. The gigantic failure and its cost, one hundred thousand casualties, will become history.

Brains, not bravery, win battles. From the Persian wars to the present day the best military condemn the inauguration of secondary campaigns that weaken the main forces operating on the decisive point. Think what those hundred thousand casualties might have gained in Flanders.

Regrets are idle. All that can be done is to remedy the past. How is this best accomplished?

Since Bulgaria has made its sordid choice, panic has invaded certain English circles. The talk is about a threat against Egypt, the Berlin to Baghdad railroad, the rape of India If the Censor had the confidence of the people he could quickly kill such silly gossip. The British Empire is not tottering.

Some talk as if the German advance through Serbia were an accomplished fact. There is no gainsaying the situation is serious, but it is far from being as hopeless as the pessimists think.

Unless some later factor appears that reveals the necessity of the entrance of Von Mackensen's armies into Serbia, I think German strategy has over-reached itself. The spoilers, in their hope to rob the granaries of the Balkans and recruit their losses from this part of the world, weaken the circle of steel that guards Germany. If that circle can be cut at any point it may mean the end. The German line is becoming more and more attenuated.

But the Bulgarian diversion may have a deeper significance. Is it a trap? What counter move do the Germans expect the Allies to take? Let us take thought.

It can be accepted as certain that the German General Staff know the whole truth about the situation in the Dardanelles. They know that the Mediterranean Expeditionary Force must be withdrawn or it will be exterminated. If it is withdrawn, it returns to the Western battle line. At the present moment Germany has her hands full in that zone. She must prevent this completely organised army from reinforcing Sir John French. Once already the Allies have been distracted from the theatre of main operations. The German General Staff ask themselves: Can this manoeuver be repeated with success? King Ferdinand is paid his price, and the experiment is made.

The German push into Serbia has for one of its objects the immobilising of the large British Force concentrated at the Dardanelles bases. By the attack on Serbia Germany hopes to draw those troops into the Balkan theatre of war and so destroy their usefulness against the main objective.

They also count on the French committing themselves largely to the Servian campaign. German spies have long ago carried the information to Berlin that France has been aiding the Serbia Army to the limit permitted by her own needs. It is also known how England has been helping the plucky mountaineer nation. Under the circumstances the Germans are right in expecting the Allies to send supports to the Serbians.

43

Again the Germans are taking advantage of the characteristic sense of honour and sentiment of the French and English. The enemy reckon that the Allies will not desert a friend in necessity.

In this they are right. The landing at Salonika is the prompt answer to the German challenge. To seize and hold this post was the first military command. How this preliminary movement is to be followed up is the next question to which we must give the most serious thought.

No war was won on sentiment. The pure material sides of all questions must hold the mind of the commanding General to the exclusion of all else. An impulse that may ruin a cause cannot be indulged.

The heroism of Serbia is epic. The struggles she has made against overwhelming odds and against pestilence has won this nation the sympathy of the world. But this sympathy must not lead the Allies to play into the hands of the Germans.

The third Balkan ·war is only in its initial stages. No man can state with certainty what action future developments may demand. But from all that lies on the table it is highly improbable that the Great War will be ended by any action in the troubled peninsula

What is here advocated the cynics will say means leaving the Balkans to settle their own fate, and deserting an ally in her extremity. If we pause to analyse the conditions of the problem, it is apparent that such is not the case. Holding Salonika as a base makes it possible to keep the Serbians supplied with the sinews of war. If the Salonika-Uskub-Nish railroad can be held, the Serbian army can be counted upon to hold back the German aggression for some time. It may even be advisable to send a small force to help maintain this line. But a large scale expedition that means denuding the Western front would be the height of folly.

When Germany is finally defeated the boundaries of the Balkan States can be re-adjusted. This is a secondary problem, and one that must not be allowed to delay the final result. And if this war is to end in something more than an inconclusive draw, Germany will have to be beaten in France and Flanders. Whenever pressure is brought to bear in this zone the far-flung German corps fly back to it like springs suddenly released. But if the Teuton Staff can induce its opponents to exhaust their energies in other fields the lost section of France and Belgium will never be recovered.

Whenever a basic principle of strategy is outraged, nine times out of ten a manoeuvre fails. It is the soundest strategy to concentrate all efforts on one objective. By such a path all military geniuses have achieved success.

Every colony is giving England of their sons ungrudgingly. Australia, New Zealand, Canada have loyally rallied to the standard. But will they continue to do so if the colonists begin to think that their sacrifices are vain, the lives of their sons squandered?

The Dardanelles disaster has brought a crisis in the war. At the same time it has taught a lesson. That lesson well learned spells victory.

45

www.ingramcontent.com/pod-product-compliance
Ingram Content Group UK Ltd.
Pitfield, Milton Keynes, MK11 3LW, UK
UKHW031004240225
455493UK00012B/1041